Dot to Dot
IN THE Sky

Also available in this series:

Dot to Dot in the Sky: Stories in the Stars

Dot to Dot in the Sky: Stories of the Planets

Dot TO Dot IN THE Sky

STORIES OF THE MOON

Joan Marie Galat

illustrations by
Lorna Bennett

whitecap

For additional information, please contact Whitecap Books Ltd.,
351 Lynn Avenue, North Vancouver, British Columbia,
Canada V7J 2C4.

Edited by Elizabeth McLean
Cover design by Roberta Batchelor
Interior layout by Roberta Batchelor

Printed and bound in Canada

Library and Archives Canada Cataloguing in Publication

Galat, Joan Marie, 1963–
        Dot to dot in the sky : stories of the moon / Joan Marie
Galat ; illustrations by Lorna Bennett.

Includes index.
ISBN 1-55285-610-0

        1. Moon—Folklore—Juvenile literature. 2. Moon—Juvenile
literature. I. Bennett, Lorna, 1960– II. Title.

QB582.G34 2004   j398.26   C2004-904485-0

The publisher acknowledges the support of the Canada Council for
the Arts and the Cultural Services Branch of the Government of British
Columbia for our publishing program. We acknowledge the financial
support of the Government of Canada through the Book Publishing
Industry Development Program for our publishing activities.

Acknowledgments

Special thanks for the generous gift of time and
assistance given by Douglas Hube, professor emeritus at the
University of Alberta and former national president (1994–96)
of the Royal Astronomical Society of Canada.
— J.M.G.

Thank you to the following people for their generous support,
technical expertise, and some modeling: Kwasi Amenu-Tekaa;
Lily Noye; Jamison Russell (Ana'soyi); Anne, Amanda, and
Austyn Locke; Perry Shulak; Chris Caldwell; Erin and Bev Chaba;
Joan Marie Galat; Amy Hinz; Matthew Hinz; and Grant Wiens . . .
and to the irreplaceable N.C. Wyeth, for inspiration.
— L.B.

Contents

MOON FACTS

Moon Myths from around the World

Throughout history, the Moon has challenged our imaginations. Cultures around the world have looked up in awe at the Moon's white orb and told stories based on what they could see with the naked eye. Across continents, the Moon has represented men, women, and animals. Some looked up and saw a rabbit in the shaded areas; others imagined frogs. Some of the characters were simple folk, others royalty. The Moon has inspired myths, folklore, and superstition. It has been worshipped, as well as held responsible for the odd behavior of people. The Moon's influence causes our tides, its phases help us mark time, its beauty captures our hearts.

Ancient people created myths to explain the mysteries of the world around them—the weather, the seasons, and the origins of nature. Their observations of the Moon and the stories they told allow us a glimpse into the minds of long-ago cultures. The myths take us back to a time when people struggled to make sense of the physical world. Some stories have morals, many reflect human struggles, and others describe the relationship between the Moon and other night sky objects.

For eons, people have looked up at the Moon and longed to explore its surface. In 1969, this dream became a reality when the Moon was first visited by American astronauts. In spite of the knowledge gained from Moon exploration, the awe inspired by our closest celestial neighbor remains intense. Each scientific discovery triggers more questions and the quest for scientific knowledge continues.

It is fascinating to look up at the ever changing Moon and search for the details that inspired ancient legends. Easily observed, yet ever mysterious, the Moon is as entrancing today as when the myths were first told!

The Story of Hina
Polynesian

Long ago, a woman named Hina lived in Hawaii. Hina had a talent for turning tree bark into a special kind of cloth, called tapa. She bleached and dyed the tapa, then used wooden stamps to imprint the cloth with pictures. The cloth was so well made and beautifully decorated that Hina's neighbors asked her to make tapa for them, too. Even the chief of her village insisted that his tapa be made by Hina.

Hina had to work all day to keep up with the many requests for her tapa. At first she loved her work, but eventually she became frustrated, for she had so little free time. Her son, Maui, did not help at all. Her husband, Aikanaka, did not help either. He spent his days hunting and his evenings complaining. He was bossy and expected Hina to fish for their supper, bring fresh water, and make him poi.

One morning, Hina decided she wanted to enjoy life and not work so much. She prayed to her guardian angel, Lauhuki, to guide her to a new home. She waited for a sign, but nothing happened, nothing changed. When the sun was high in the sky, Hina gave up and walked to the stream to collect fresh water in her gourds.

At the stream, Hina saw a rainbow that started in the grass but reached toward the Sun. Perhaps Lauhuki had answered her prayers! Hoping the Sun was to be her new home, she stepped onto the rainbow and began the journey upward. Hina walked for a very long time, but the closer she got to the sun, the more weary she became. Her skin turned red, her feet grew swollen, and an incredible giddiness overcame her. With a sudden lurch downward, Hina lost her footing and fell back to Earth.

Hina lay on the grass all afternoon and into the early evening. By the time she felt well enough to walk, the sun had set and moonbeams shone down upon her skin. Once again, she prayed to Lauhuki to lead her to a place where she could be happy. Hina waited and waited, but did not sense a reply. She gathered her gourds, filled them with water, and returned to the cave where she lived with Aikanaka.

As soon as Aikanaka saw Hina, he shouted for his supper. Hina ignored him and gathered her tapa-making tools into a basket. Aikanaka bellowed again for something to eat, but instead of answering, Hina took her basket and stormed out of the cave.

Hina strode back to the stream and saw the rainbow still arching skyward from the grass. Once again she stepped onto the rainbow and began to climb. Up, up she went, never looking back, until suddenly she heard shouting. Turning, she saw Aikanaka on the rainbow, trying to follow her into the sky. The rainbow was not strong enough to hold him and, just as he caught up to Hina, he began to slip down. Aikanaka tried to save himself by hanging onto Hina's ankle. She pulled it free, but was badly bruised in the spot his hand touched. Despite the pain, Hina limped onward until she finally reached the Moon.

Hina made her home on the Moon and found it so peaceful, she once again enjoyed life. If you look up, you can see the Hawaiian goddess turning bark into tapa. When rain falls, the Hawaiians say she must be sprinkling water on the cloth, and when lightning strikes, they imagine her shaking folds out of the tapa. A cloud-covered sky means Hina has spread the cloth out to dry.

Hina is a Polynesian goddess, known as the guardian of the underworld and a patroness of arts and crafts. She has also been called Ina, Sina, and Rona.

Our Closest Neighbor

- The Moon is our closest celestial neighbor and a natural satellite of Earth, held in orbit by the Earth's gravitational attraction.

- Most moons are significantly smaller than the planets they orbit, but the Earth's moon is considered large enough to resemble a double-planet system.

- As the Moon orbits Earth, it completes a cycle of phases in 29 days, 12 hours, 44 minutes, and 2.8 seconds, a time that forms the basis of our calendar month. The calendar months are not exactly the same length as the lunar cycle; they have been adjusted to fit within an Earth year of 365$\frac{1}{4}$ days.

- Normally the brightest object in our sky other than the Sun, the Moon shines by reflecting sunlight. It only reflects 7 percent of the light that strikes it, which is similar to the reflectivity of coal dust.

- Because gravity on the Moon is one-sixth weaker than on Earth, if you weighed 45 kilograms (100 pounds) on Earth, you would weigh only 7.5 kilograms (16.6 pounds) on the Moon. You would be able to jump six times higher and farther than you can on Earth.

The Greedy Man in the Moon
Chinese

A very long time ago, a mother and son lived in a simple house near a village in China. The boy often played in the forest and one day, as he walked among the trees, he saw a sparrow on the path. The little bird did not fly away when he neared, so he bent down to have a closer look. It still did not move and he saw that the bird was unable to walk or even hop.

Reaching down, the boy gently cupped the sparrow in his hands. The tiny bird did not struggle, but he could feel its heart thumping against his fingers. Taking careful steps to avoid jostling the little creature, the boy carried the bird through the forest and back to his home.

When he showed his mother the sparrow, she looked at it carefully and said, "I believe its leg is broken. Let us do whatever is needed to help it become well again." She took a soft, light cloth from a basket, ripped it into small strips, and together they wrapped the gauze around the bird's leg. The boy found a dish, filled it with water, and placed it next to the bird. He went outside to look for seeds and gathered enough to fill a small dish so the sparrow could eat whenever it felt hungry. Every day, he brought the bird fresh water and a new supply of food to help it become strong. As the weeks passed, the sparrow began to regain the use of its leg.

A new Moon came and went before the bird was finally able to carry its full weight on the leg that had been broken. The mother and son were very fond of the sparrow, but knew the time had come to let it go free. After saying good-bye, the boy placed it on his palm, and stretched his hand out the open window. The sparrow spread its wings and hopped forward before soaring up and away toward the forest. They watched until it disappeared from sight.

The next morning, the mother and son sat down near an open window to eat breakfast. Suddenly, the sparrow surprised them by landing on the windowsill with a seed in its mouth. It dropped the seed, then astonished them once more, this time by speaking! "Thank you for caring for me and looking after my wounded leg. I have returned to give you a special gift. Plant this and see what happens." Before the mother or son could ask any questions, the bird flew off into the sky.

The boy picked the seed up from the windowsill and walked out to the garden. Choosing a spot where the soil

was soft, he dug a small hole and placed the seed in the ground. He gently pushed soil over the hole and marked the spot with a twig from the forest. Every day he watered the soil, and on the third day a soft green shoot appeared.

Although the boy could tell the plant was a melon vine, it was unlike any melon he had ever seen. Its leaves were the richest green, and the plant was almost fully grown after a single week. A single, golden flower bloomed. Over the next fourteen days it turned into a golden melon.

The boy waited patiently for the melon to ripen. When it was ready, he plucked it from the vine to give to his mother. He held the melon up, and as he admired it, the fruit separated into two pieces. Inside rested a single gold coin! When he pulled the coin from the fruit, another appeared. When he reached for the second coin, another appeared, until there was a pile of gold coins at his feet.

Word of their good fortune spread. A greedy man from the village came to find out how they had become so rich. They told the man about the bird and the seed and the melon and the gold. The man's jealousy was so great, he immediately walked to the forest to look for a bird with a broken leg. Certain he was deserving of great riches, the greedy man searched the woods for several days, but he could not find a wounded bird. His impatience grew until he could stand it no more. Picking up a rock, the man took careful aim and threw the stone at a sparrow sitting on a branch. The stone hit the sparrow and the bird fell to the ground.

The greedy man ran to the sparrow and picked it up. "I will make you strong again," he told the bird, then took it home and placed it in a cage. Every day he fed and watered the bird, and each time he told it he expected to be rewarded for his efforts. Finally a new Moon had come and gone and the sparrow was well enough to be on its own. The greedy man took the bird from its cage and stood by an open window. The sparrow stared at the greedy man for a moment, then turned and flew out into the sunshine.

That night, the greedy man could not sleep, he was so excited about the money he was bound to receive. At last morning arrived, and after some time the sparrow appeared with a seed in its beak. It dropped the seed on the ground in front of the man and said, "Here is something special for you.

Plant this seed and you will get what you deserve."

The greedy man went straight to his garden and planted the seed. Every day, he carefully watered the ground and pulled out any weeds that appeared. Three days later, a melon shoot sprouted from the soil and, as the plant grew, several golden buds began to bloom. The man counted twelve flowers and laughed an evil laugh, for the boy had only grown a single blossom. "I will be the richest of all!" he chortled.

The boy's melon had grown along the ground, but the stalk of this plant grew toward the sky. In only two weeks, the vine was taller than any house. Melons hung from the highest runners and the man decided to climb the plant to reach the best-looking fruit at the top. As he climbed, the vine grew taller, until every step he took made it stretch even higher beyond the clouds.

Finally the man reached the first melon and broke the fruit apart. Instead of a gold coin, he found a wriggling worm. Frowning, he let the fruit fall and climbed until he reached another ripe melon. Seeing another worm, the man screamed in anger. He climbed and climbed, checking each melon, but each time he found another worm.

At last there was only one melon at the very top. Hand over hand, the man climbed, but the harder he tried to reach the melon, the faster the plant grew. It stretched higher and higher until at last the fruit came to rest on the Moon. The man leaped onto the Moon's surface and grabbed the melon, certain he would at last be rich, but again there was only a worm.

As he shook his fist at the useless melon, the plant withered and fell away behind him, leaving no way to get back to Earth. If you look carefully, you can still see the face of the greedy man in the Moon.

THE MOON'S ORIGIN

- Scientists are not sure how the Moon evolved, but the "big splash" theory is popular. It suggests that a Mars-sized space object hit Earth at a high speed. Molten material from the two bodies could have formed a ring of particles around Earth, and eventually come together to form the Moon. Other theories say the Moon could have formed alongside Earth, or come from elsewhere and been captured by Earth's gravity.

- By studying and dating lunar rock samples, scientists discovered the Moon is 4.6 billion years old.

PHASES OF THE MOON

- Half the Moon is in sunlight while the other half is dark, just like Earth. The shape of the Moon appears to change as it goes around Earth, depending how much of the sunlit side is visible. This is why we see different phases of the Moon.

- The Moon has eight named phases, although there is a smooth and continuous change from one phase to the next.

  1. **New Moon:** We cannot see the Moon because it is between the Sun and Earth, and its unlit side faces Earth.

  2. **Waxing Crescent:** The sunlit portion facing Earth grows in size.

  3. **First Quarter:** Half of the sunlit portion can be seen. The Moon has finished the first quarter of its orbit.

  4. **Waxing Gibbous:** About three-quarters of the Moon is now visible.

  5. **Full Moon:** The entire sunlit portion of the Moon can be seen.

  6. **Waning Gibbous:** The portion of the sunlit side of the Moon facing Earth becomes smaller, with about three-quarters visible.

  7. **Last Quarter:** Half of the sunlit portion can be seen. Three-quarters of the monthly orbit is complete.

  8. **Waning Crescent:** Less than half of the Earth-facing side of the Moon is illuminated.

- The Earth, Moon, and Sun are in line during the Full Moon and New Moon phases.

Observing Moon Phases

- The Moon always rises in the east and sets in the west.

- The phases most often observed occur during the two weeks after New Moon, from Crescent through First Quarter to Full Moon. The Moon at waxing Crescent to First Quarter appears in the western sky at sunset. The First Quarter rises in the east at noon. It is above the horizon for half the daytime hours, but is often only noticed when the darkening sky makes it more obvious.

- Sometimes in the fall, the rising Full Moon appears unusually large when it is near the horizon. This is an illusion that occurs because of the way the brain processes images. The Moon at this time is called the "harvest moon" or "hunter's moon."

- You can often see the Moon during the day, but you will never see a Full Moon high in the sky in the daytime. To see the Moon in the morning after sunrise, pick a day when it is close to its last quarter.

Rabbit and the Moon Man

Canadian Mi'k Maq

A very long time ago, Rabbit lived in a remote forest, far away from any people. Rabbit was a superb hunter. He set traps to catch birds and small animals, such as mice and squirrels, and shared this food with his grandmother. Rabbit's snares were never empty, so the two rabbits always went to sleep well fed. They had no worries at all, until one winter, day after day, Rabbit found his traps empty.

Rabbit and Grandmother became very hungry. It seemed the two would starve unless they could figure out why the traps no longer worked. Rabbit inspected the snow for tracks and saw that animals and birds had stepped into his snares. He realized animals were still getting caught, but someone was stealing from the snares. He tried visiting the traps at different times, but no matter when he checked they were always empty.

Rabbit had no idea who the thief might be, but he refused to give up. He got up earlier and earlier every morning, but each time the traps had already been emptied. He could not figure out how to catch the thief and became more and more frustrated.

Very early one morning, Rabbit stepped outside into a fresh layer of snow. He hopped down the trail to the part of the forest near the stream where his snares were set. Rabbit discovered fresh tracks unlike any he had ever seen before! The marks in the snow were long and narrow, but oddest of all, they were pale—like the light of the Moon.

Rabbit ran home and told Grandmother what he had found, but she did not know what could have made the tracks. He decided to stay up all night and see if he could catch the thief. Taking some bowstring, Rabbit twisted, looped, and twirled the strands until he had made a snare tough enough to hold the strongest of creatures. He laid the snare near the other traps, and stretched the end of the bowstring to a clump of trees.

That night, Rabbit came back to the traps. It was a calm, cold night, with no clouds to warm the Earth's air. He hid among the trees and grasped the end of the bowstring in his paws, hoping he would be strong enough to pull the string tight if the thief stepped into the snare. Rabbit knew he might have to stay awake all night. He tried to ignore the flip-flops in his stomach by gazing at the twinkling stars and shining Moon. After some time, it became so dark Rabbit could not even see the string in his paws. He looked up to see if clouds had blown in, but there was no wind. To Rabbit's amazement, the stars were still in the sky but the Moon had disappeared!

Lip twitching nervously and feet itching to take off down the path, Rabbit forced himself to stay in his hiding place. In a little while, his patience was rewarded. Someone was walking down the trail toward his traps! The creature glowed with a light so bright, Rabbit could not make out its shape.

Rabbit tightly gripped the string in his paw and watched the creature come closer and closer. When the moment was right, Rabbit pulled the bow-string with such a mighty effort, it held the thief snug. He wrapped the other end of the bowstring around the tree, making sure the glowing creature was tied fast to the trunk.

Its light was so intense now, poor Rabbit became even more frightened. Instead of looking to see what he had caught, Rabbit ran home to Grandmother and

told her the creature with the long foot was tied to a tree. She told him to go back and order it not to rob the traps anymore. Rabbit wanted to wait and go in the daylight, but Grandmother insisted he must not wait.

Rabbit sped back to the forest, slowing when he drew closer to the snare. The light was so strong he could not look directly at the creature. Eyes sore and red, he leaned over the stream to splash water on his face, but the icy water did not help. Rabbit decided to try to dim the light. He scooped up handfuls of snow and threw them at the creature, but the snow sizzled and melted when it hit, then fell to the ground in rivulets of water.

Rabbit was tired and scared. He was also hungry, for he had not had a good meal in a long time. With a sudden surge of anger and frustration, Rabbit reached down into the stream and brought up two big handfuls of black mud. He brought his paws together to make the mud into a ball and threw it with all his strength at the light. The mud ball hit with a thud, and the creature cried out, "Stop! I am the Moon Man and I must return to the sky before the Sun appears. Untie me at once or I will kill you!"

Rabbit shook with fear. Too afraid to even answer, Rabbit ran back to his grandmother. When she heard his tale, she also became frightened. "Run!" she told him. "Run as fast as you can and let the Moon Man go before the Sun rises."

Rabbit ran back into the forest, but stopped some distance from the light. Lips quivering, he shouted, "I will let you go, Moon Man, but promise you will never steal our food again and never return to Earth."

"I promise!" shouted the Moon Man. "As long as you let me go before the Sun shows its face! Quickly now!"

Rabbit came closer to the trap, blinking rapidly to shield his eyes from the light. He leaned close to cut the snare with his teeth, scorching his shoulders in the process. The Moon Man hurried away as soon as he was free, for the eastern sky was already tinted with the coming Sun.

The Moon Man kept his promise and never returned. He still lights the Earth as he travels across the night sky, but every month the Moon Man disappears for a few days. He goes to a lonely place to try to wash off the mud. No matter how hard he tries, the Moon Man cannot get rid of the mud and carries its imprint today.

Rabbit never found his snares emptied again, but to this day he has pink eyes and a scorch-marked coat. He still blinks a lot and his lips still quiver, reminding him of that brave night when he caught the Moon Man and banished him from Earth.

CRATERS

Most craters formed during a period beginning around 4 billion years ago when the impact of meteorites punctured the Moon's crust. About a billion years later, the onslaught lessened, ending with a small number of large impacts. Seeping lava eventually filled these depressions. As the lava solidified, smooth lowland plains called maria were formed.

Space debris strikes the Moon's surface directly instead of burning up because the Moon does not have an atmosphere like Earth does.

The Buried Moon
English

Long ago, there was a place in England where the marshy bogs and swamps were haunted with horrors—wicked goblins, ghosts, witches, will-o'-the-wisps, and black cats. They were evil beings who lived to make trouble and especially delighted in scaring people who crossed the swamps. Everyone was afraid to go near the brackish water, in case they were tricked into stepping into quicksand or pools of mud.

Being creatures of the night, the horrors always attacked in complete darkness. The only time it was safe to cross the bog was when the Moon was out. The Moon knew about the evil creatures and gave up her own rest to shine her light into the darkest corners of the bog.

Night after night, the Moon cast her light, but after some time began to wonder if the bog was really such a dangerous place. She decided to go down to Earth and see for herself.

The Moon waited until the part of the month when her brightness was hidden and the sky was naturally dark. She concealed her long glimmering hair with a black hood, covered herself in a black cape, and allowed herself to float downward until her feet touched the Earth.

The Moon landed next to a green stream trickling into a pool of black water. She worked her way over spongy grasses that oozed and squirted slime, finally reaching a rocky path. The night was inky black except for a bit of radiance escaping from the Moon's feet and the faint reflection of starlight in the water. There was barely enough light for her to make out the twisted and bent trees eerily creaking in the wind. The Moon made her way deeper into the cheerless bog, searching for the horrors that were said to live there.

Gradually the Moon's eyes became accustomed to the dark. She began to notice movement in the bog and realized with a start that witches were jeering as she passed. Eyes from unseen creatures watched every step, while other frightening horrors crawled closer and closer.

The Moon tried to walk faster, but a tree root rose from the ground and made her lose her footing. Almost falling into the water, she tried to steady herself by grabbing the nearest tree branch. As soon as she touched the tree, the limb wrapped itself tightly around her wrist. Heart pounding, the Moon pulled and pulled, but her efforts were in vain. Soon both her

Moon Geology

- The Moon has a rocky crust 60 to 100 kilometres (40 to 60 miles) thick. The mountain ranges around some large craters and maria formed as a result of material thrown from the impact site, as well as from crust uplifting.

- Most of the Moon is covered with soil, called regolith, a mixture of fine dust and rocky debris created when meteoroids, comets, and asteroids struck the Moon's surface.

- Moon rocks range in age from about 3.2 billion years in the maria to almost 4.6 billion years in the highlands.

- The youngest rocks on the Moon are about as old as the oldest rocks on Earth because erosion and plate tectonics change the Earth's surface, but the Moon's surface remains virtually undisturbed. The Moon provides a history of the first billion years, which may be shared by the terrestrial or inner planets—Mercury, Venus, Earth, and Mars.

hands were caught and held so tightly it was impossible to get free.

The witches jeered and the other horrors cackled and cawed with glee as they crawled closer and closer. The Moon watched them with growing fear and wished she had never come down to Earth. Suddenly the witches and horrors turned away. Looking down the path, the Moon heard the squishing sound of someone running through the marsh.

Twisting her head to see what was coming, she made out the grimacing, frightened face of a man, panting in exhaustion as he tried to escape the bog. He had been wandering aimlessly when he spotted the bit of light that escaped from the Moon's feet. Thinking he had found a way out, the unfortunate man ran toward the light, not knowing he was heading straight into the path of the horrors.

The Moon felt terrible. She knew if she had not come to the bog, the man would not be in such danger. In a final act of desperation, she struggled to free herself. As the Moon twisted and turned, the hood slipped from her head and the light from her shining white hair lit up the bog. The evil beings screamed and scattered, but the man let out a joyous holler. He had spotted the path leading out of the bog and was already running home. If he had taken the time to look back, he would have seen the evil beings withdraw deep into the bog, frightened by the light.

Although the Moon was happy to see the man escape, she desperately wanted to be free. She struggled against the tree's grip, but still could not get loose. Exhausted, the Moon collapsed to the ground. As she fell, her hood dropped over her hair, once again leaving the bog in darkness.

The witches and goblins and evil beings did not wait to see if it would stay dark. They rushed toward the fallen Moon, yelling and screaming and arguing about her fate. The Moon struggled to shield herself, but they yanked her from the grip of the tree and pushed her down deep into a black pool of water. Now she was truly caught, for the horrors rolled a long rectangular stone over her to keep her down. Two will-o'-the-wisps were given the job of making sure the Moon did not rise again.

No one realized the Moon was missing until the evening came when she should have crossed the sky. The people did not know what to make of her disappearance or how to safely cross the bog without the Moon's help. The evil horrors became more brazen as each dark night passed.

The people living near the bog had no idea how to solve this problem. They became so alarmed, they decided to visit the Wise Woman and ask her for advice. They crossed the village to reach her home and knocked on her door. The Wise Woman welcomed them inside and listened to their tale, but did not answer their questions right away. Instead, she opened a book and searched through its pages. Next, she stared down into the depths of her cauldron. Finally, she turned her eyes to a special mirror and gazed into it for several minutes.

GRAVITY AND TIDES

- Gravity from the Moon and Sun causes ocean tides. The tidal effect of the Moon is twice as large as the tidal effect of the Sun, since it is so much closer to Earth. Twice a day, water rises, then falls as bulges of tidal water follow the Moon's orbit around Earth. Because the gravitational attraction of the Moon on the side of the Earth nearest it is stronger than the attraction on the opposite side of the Earth, Earth actually stretches toward the Moon. The solid Earth stretches by a very slight amount, but the oceans stretch by a noticeable amount, producing two tidal bulges.

- Tides arrive about 50 minutes later each day.

- Continuous tidal movement and tidal friction slow the Earth's rotation very slightly, increasing day length by about 2.3 milliseconds every century.

- The height of a tide depends on the position of the Moon in its orbit, as well as on the geography of the coastline.

- The lowest low tides and the highest high tides are called spring tides. They happen during a New Moon or Full Moon, when the Sun, Earth, and Moon are directly in line. There are two spring (New and Full Moon) and two neap (Quarter phase) tides each month.

- Neap tides are the lowest high tides and the highest low tides. They occur when the Sun's gravity counteracts some of the Moon's tidal pull. This happens when the Sun is at a right angle to the Moon, during the Moon's First and Last Quarter phases.

Hats in their hands, the people from the bog waited respectfully for the Wise Woman to share her thoughts. When at last she spoke, she said only, "I do not know what happened to the Moon."

More time passed and the horrors of the night became even bolder. Their screams and chants sounded louder and closer as each night passed. The people who lived near the bog became so afraid, they would no longer even travel near the edge of the marshy land.

They spent hour after hour, day after day trying to guess what might have happened to the Moon. Many nights were spent sharing stories of how the Moon had saved each of them from different horrors. One evening, the last man to cross the bog told the tale of what had happened the night he lost his way. As the man spoke, he realized the light he had seen might have come from the Moon.

With great excitement, the villagers returned to the Wise Woman and repeated the story of the brilliant light on the ground. She gazed once more into her book, cauldron, and mirror.

Finally the Wise Woman spoke. "Go to the bog with hazel twigs in your hands. Put a rock in your mouth to make sure you do not talk, then walk deep into the bog. You must search for a cross, a coffin, and a candle."

That night, some of the villagers gathered, put rocks in their mouths, carried hazel twigs, and silently walked deeper and deeper into the bog, searching for the cross, the coffin, and the candle. It was very hard for them not to talk or cry out as the horrors silently brushed by and the tree branches prodded them.

Eventually they came to a pool where a great rock jutted out. It looked just like a coffin! The tree branches hanging over the bog were formed into a cross and two will-o'-the-wisps glimmered like candle flames. The men gathered close and leaned over the water to lift the stone. They heaved with all their might until the rock shifted and they saw the Moon's smiling face. The Moon glittered and gleamed, then rose up in such brilliance they were forced to turn away from her light.

The horrors, goblins, and witches in the bog scattered, the trees stopped prodding the villagers, and the night became safe as the Moon rose back to her place in the sky. Radiant, happy, and as kind as ever, the Moon still shines her light to protect the people who saved her from the horrors of the bog.

LUNAR ECLIPSES

- A lunar eclipse occurs when the Earth's shadow falls upon the Moon. There are three types of eclipses:

  1. A **penumbral eclipse** occurs when the Full Moon passes through a partially shadowed area that surrounds the Earth's inner, darker shadow.

  2. A **total umbral eclipse** occurs when a Full Moon moves through the umbra—the darkest part of the Earth's shadow.

  3. A **partial umbral eclipse** occurs when some of the Moon is in the umbra, and the rest is in the penumbra.

- It can take up to four hours for the Moon to fully pass through the shadow. Totality, the period when the Moon is fully in the shadow, may last more than an hour and a half.

- Two to five lunar eclipses occur every year. There will be 230 lunar eclipses during the 21st century. It is safe and easy to observe a lunar eclipse.

- We do not have a lunar eclipse every month because most of the time the Full Moon passes above or below the Earth's shadow.

Observing Lunar Eclipses

- The Moon will appear darker during an umbral eclipse, but can also be colorful if hit with indirect sunlight that has been refracted (bent) through Earth's atmosphere. When the blue light is scattered, the redder light reaches the Moon, causing the eclipsed Moon to appear dark brown or red.

- The amount of cloud and dust in the Earth's atmosphere affects the darkness of the Moon during an eclipse, as well as its color. Lunar eclipses appear especially dark after large volcanic eruptions have spewed ash into our atmosphere.

- Penumbral eclipses are difficult to detect even with a telescope, but partial and total umbral eclipses are easy to see with the unaided eye. You don't need protective filters or even a telescope. Binoculars with a magnification of 7x35 or 7x50 can be used to enlarge the view and make the edge of the shadow and the red coloration easier to see.

- When skies are clear, everyone on the night side of Earth can observe a lunar eclipse.

The Moon Princess
Japanese

Long ago, a kind old bamboo cutter and his wife lived at the base of a mountain in Japan. Every morning, the man climbed up a ridge to an ancient forest where he spent the hours chopping bamboo. One day, the man noticed a bamboo tree glowing with a mysterious light. He cut the wood apart to see why it shone so strangely. Within the bamboo was a most enchanting baby girl, small enough to fit in his hand. The bamboo cutter gently picked up the child and carried her down the mountain to his wife. They rejoiced, thanking the mysteries of heaven for the miracle of a child to love.

They named their new daughter Kaguya Hime, which means Princess of Light. The next day, the kind old woman took care of Kaguya while the bamboo cutter climbed the mountain to the ancient forest. Once again he found a bamboo tree glowing with golden light. When he cut it down, pieces of gold fell to the ground. Every day after that, the old man found another glowing bamboo tree, each one filled with gold.

The bamboo cutter and his wife used the gold to care for Kaguya. They bought her fine silk kimonos and made sure she had everything she could possibly need.

Kaguya grew quickly, changing from an infant to a beautiful young lady in only three months. She was so enchanting, all the bamboo cutter had to do was glance at her whenever he felt frustrated or sad and his spirits would be restored. Her beauty was so great, a special glow seemed to radiate from her skin. It filled the bamboo cutter's house with so much light, all shadows disappeared and they no longer needed to brighten their home with lamps.

Word of Kaguya's beauty spread. After some time, the bamboo cutter told her it was time to choose a man to be her husband. He wanted to see Kaguya married so that he would know there was someone to look after her when he became too old.

Many young men came to call, each wishing to win her hand in marriage. Among the suitors were five famous and wealthy princes. Each one wrote Kaguya a letter asking for a chance to show his love, but she would not even reply. They pestered the bamboo cutter to make her marry until finally he asked her to choose the man she thought would treat her most kindly.

Kaguya did not want to get married, but to please the bamboo cutter she thought about her father's request before answering. At last she said,

"I do not know these men. I do not know who is the most handsome or the most wealthy. I will choose the one who will prove that he wants me the most." She agreed to marry whichever man could bring her what she asked, but cleverly requested gifts that would be almost impossible to find. She hoped that failure would make them give up and leave her alone.

Kaguya asked the first prince to go to India and return with the begging bowl used by Buddha.

She asked the second prince to bring her a branch from a rare tree, known to have silver leaves and gold stems. The tree could only be found on a sacred mountain beyond the sea.

She asked the third prince for a jeweled fur from the fire animal, with hair so lustrous it would not burn if put into a fire.

She asked the fourth to get the Dragon King's necklace, which had an amazing pearl that shimmered blue, red, yellow, green, and black.

She asked the fifth for a perfect cowry shell from the belly of a swallow, as well as the bird, alive and well.

The first prince wanted to have Kaguya for his wife, but he did not want to go all the way to India looking for the Buddha's begging bowl. He pretended to get a boat ready to sail across the ocean, but when no one was looking the prince hid in the mountains. He waited several months before finally returning with a bowl taken from a hilltop temple. The bowl was presented to Kaguya, who immediately pronounced it a fake. The bowl was dirty and did not have the special glow that would prove it genuine. Shamed, the prince hung his head and walked away.

The second prince took one servant and set out to sea. He waited until it was dark, then returned to port and arranged for six craftsmen to make a jeweled branch of gold and silver. The jewelers worked for many days and nights until they had made a branch more beautiful than any object imaginable. The prince took the branch and secretly sailed out of the harbor, returning the next morning as if he were back from a very long journey. He went straight to Kaguya's home and presented her with the branch.

When Kaguya saw the exquisite gold and silver, her heart filled with dread. She knew she had no choice but to keep her promise and was about to accept his marriage proposal when there came an angry pounding on the door. The bamboo cutter opened the door and the six craftsmen surrounded the prince, demanding to be paid for their work. With great relief, Kaguya sent the deceiving prince away for good.

The third prince was very rich. He sent a servant out with a bag of gold, instructing him to find the legendary jeweled fur and return with it. After much searching, the servant found the fur but did not have enough money to buy it. The prince sent more money and finally the servant returned with a lustrous fur, decorated with precious jewels. The ecstatic prince rushed to the bamboo cutter's house and presented the fur to Kaguya. She held the heavy fur in dismay, certain she would now be forced to become a bride.

"I have one last request before I agree to be married," Kaguya told the prince. "If this is really the fur of the fire animal, it will not burn when thrown upon a flame." The prince and the bamboo cutter turned pale and tried to reason with Kaguya. "Surely you can see from the fur's beauty it is genuine," they argued, but she insisted on proof with the words, "Let us do it." The fur was thrown upon the hearth and disappeared into ashes and smoke. Kaguya felt badly because she knew the prince had thought the fur was genuine, but still she sent him away.

The fourth suitor commanded his servants to go forth, fight the dragon, and return with the multicolored pearl necklace. His men did not want to risk their lives, but the prince was so insistent they tired of arguing with him. The servants took the money, divided it amongst themselves, and ran off in different directions. When the servants did not return, the prince realized he had been deserted. He was so angry, he decided to fight the dragon himself.

Gathering his bow and arrow, the prince called to his sailing crew and set forth in search of the Dragon King. The sea was calm at the beginning of the voyage, but after some time thunderclouds darkened the sky. Rain poured from the heavens and immense waves crashed against the gunwales in the worst storm the sailors had ever seen. They thought the sea god knew of their mission and was trying to split the boat in half to show his anger. Fearing death, the prince gave up his quest for the multicolored pearl necklace and the sea became calm once more. The sorrowful prince returned home empty-handed, with no hope of marrying Kaguya.

The fifth prince did not know how to get a cowry shell from the belly of a swallow. He decided to ask for advice from a wise man, who told him to look for the shell when the swallow was laying her eggs.

On his way home, the prince noticed several swallows perching on top of the walls of his palace. Clinging to the walls were nests of mud. The prince ordered his servants to build a basket large enough to reach the nests. When the basket was ready, the prince climbed in and held tight. The servants hoisted him skyward until he could touch the lowest nest. The prince stretched his arm into the nest and immediately felt something smooth and round. He put it into his pocket and, clinging to the basket, shouted to be lowered.

The servants pulled the rope with a tug so hard, the rope snapped and the prince fell to the ground. Bruised and sore, he reached into his pocket and saw he held only a plain swallow's egg. Too injured to keep looking for a cowry shell, the prince was forced to give up.

Since none of the princes was able to satisfy Kaguya, she continued to live peacefully with the bamboo cutter and his wife. Four years passed without incident, until one night the kind old couple found Kaguya looking up at the Moon and crying. They begged her to tell them what was making her so sad. Kaguya told them she was a princess from the Moon who had been sent to Earth for protection. There had been a war, but now it was over and safe to return. On the next full Moon, which would be the fifteenth night of August, the people of the Moon would come to take her home.

The frightened bamboo cutter could not bear the thought of losing the daughter he loved so much. He asked the emperor for help. The emperor sent 2000 samurai to protect her and, on the fifteenth of August, the warriors were ready with bows and arrows. When the sun set, Kaguya was in her room with the door and windows firmly locked. On the roof and in the garden, samurai drew their bowstrings taut as the Moon rose up into the sky. Moonlight bathed the Earth, until at midnight a cloud of light rose from the moonbeams and the sky began to shine with a majestic light. As the light touched the samurai, they became paralyzed and the door to Kaguya's room opened.

Kaguya stepped onto the cloud of light and bade her parents a sad and loving farewell. She rose upward, crying as she disappeared from sight. The flickering lights of her teardrops can still be seen today. Known as tears of love from the Moon, they are also sometimes called fireflies.

MOON TALES

- Many cultures see a picture when they look at the Full Moon. Some see a face, often called "The Man in the Moon." Others see a human figure: sometimes a man; sometimes a woman, a man and woman together, or a woman with a child. Others say there is a blacksmith with an anvil and hammer, the dirty handmarks of a mischievous boy, or an owl holding a club.

- In ancient China, the Moon was called the Pearl of Heaven.

- In Siberia, the Yakut people look up at the Moon and imagine a girl carrying two buckets.

- In British Columbia, the Lillooet Native people traditionally say the spots on the Moon are two frogs sitting on the Moon's face.

- The South African Hottentots tell a story about a hare who hopped up to the Moon. They say you can still see him and his paw tracks.

- The expression "once in a blue moon" refers to something that does not happen very often. In a month with two Full Moons, the second is called a "blue moon." This happens about once every three years because there are about $12\frac{1}{3}$ lunar cycles each year. It takes the Moon 29.5 days to complete its phases, but 11 of the 12 months have 30 or 31 days, so eventually two Full Moons occur in the same month.

- The word lunatic comes from *luna*, the Latin word for moon. Some people think the Full Moon has an effect on behavior, and makes people act foolish or crazy.

Artemis, Goddess of the Moon

Artemis was the daughter of Zeus and Leto, as well as twin sister to Apollo. She was called the goddess of the chase because of her love of hunting. Although she was very beautiful, Artemis was not like most other goddesses. She had no interest in men or marriage and preferred to spend her time roaming the wild countryside.

One day, Zeus gave Apollo a gift. It was a golden chariot with white horses and a golden bow with golden arrows. Apollo had the task of carrying the Sun across the sky in his chariot, and was known as the god of the Sun. Zeus wanted to give Artemis a present also, but was not sure what would please his daughter. He asked Artemis what would bring her happiness. She asked for a chariot like her brother's, but in silver, as well as a silver hunting dress, a bow with arrows, and a pack of hunting dogs. She also wanted twenty wood nymphs and twenty water nymphs to keep her company and do her bidding.

Zeus agreed to her requests and put the gods to work. Hephaestus, the blacksmith god, was told to direct the Cyclops, the one-eyed giants, to make a bow with arrows. Pan, the shepherd god, was asked to supply Artemis with hounds. The goddess was allowed to choose her own nymphs.

Artemis was anxious to go hunting, but could not leave until she found the best way to pull her new chariot. She ordered two of her dogs to go into the mountains and bring back a strong, healthy deer. Running and yelping, they returned herding two stags with tremendous antlers. Artemis harnessed the deer to her silver chariot and rode into the mountain wilderness. At night, the goddess of the Moon pulled the bright orb across the sky.

Artemis spent her days hunting for the gods with arms so steady and aim so true, she could shoot a tree in half. When tired from hunting, she relaxed in the forest at a cave beside a sacred spring of clear water. One day, thinking she was alone with the woodland nymphs, Artemis decided to bathe in the spring. She gave her bow and arrows to the nymphs, took off her robe and sandals, and waded into the water. She did not know that a hunter called Actaeon was wandering the forest nearby with his dogs.

Weary of the chase, Actaeon had left his friends to continue their hunt without him. He walked through the forest along the same trail that led to the spring where Artemis splashed in

Nearside of the Moon

- The same side of the Moon, the nearside, always faces Earth because the Moon takes the same amount of time to spin on its axis as it does to orbit Earth. Imagine the Earth as a round table, and yourself as the Moon, facing the table as you circle it.

- All spacecraft landings have occurred on the Moon's nearside, so that communication can take place with Mission Control on Earth.

- Maria are more common on the nearside of the Moon.

the water. Reaching the spring, Actaeon spotted the goddess and stood completely still, mesmerized by her beauty. Artemis was embarrassed to be seen by a mortal and became so enraged she splashed water onto Actaeon's face.

When the drops hit Actaeon, his skin became fur, his feet turned to hooves, and his head sprouted antlers. Now a frightened and confused stag, Actaeon tried to run away, but his dogs were trained to follow running deer. They chased after him, barking and snapping until they caught their master and brought him down. Unable to command his dogs to stop, Actaeon's life ended in the forest.

Another story tells about Artemis and Orion, the hunter. Although Artemis had no wish to marry, she enjoyed spending time with Orion. He was a very good hunter and never boasted. Artemis and Orion spent so much time together hunting goats on the island of Crete that the goddess stopped driving the Moon across the sky in her silver chariot. Apollo reminded her over and over not to ignore the Moon, but Artemis would not listen.

Apollo became so angry he decided to teach Artemis a lesson. He used his power to shield Orion in light, then challenged his sister to shoot an arrow into the brightness. She could not resist showing off and immediately aimed an arrow into the light, not knowing it concealed Orion as he swam in the sea.

When the waves brought Orion's body to shore, Artemis was heartbroken. She pulled him into the Moon chariot and rode high into the sky, where the great hunter turned into stars. She took him to the darkest part of the sky where he would shine brightly forever.

The Moon goddess is known by several names. Diana is her Roman name. She is also called Cynthia, Delia, Hecate, Luna, Phoebe, and Selene. She is the patroness of unmarried girls and chastity. Artemis was sometimes also called the Mistress of the Beasts, for she had a special power over wild animals, particularly bears.

MOON EXPLORATION

- The Moon was first explored with unmanned spacecraft. Lunar probes took pictures of the Moon from orbit, while others took pictures before crashing into its surface. In 1966, the first craft landed on the Moon—the Russian Luna 9.

- In the United States, the National Aeronautics and Space Administration, called NASA, had developed the Apollo program to send humans to the Moon.

- Apollo 8 was the first manned spacecraft to leave Earth's gravity and approach the Moon. In 1968, Apollo 8 astronauts circled the Moon 10 times.

- The first astronauts walked on the Moon in July 1969. It took the Apollo 11 crew four days, six hours, and 45 minutes to reach the Moon from Cape Canaveral, Florida.

- When the Apollo spacecraft entered the Moon's orbit, the lunar module separated from the command module. One astronaut circled the Moon in the command module, while the other two landed on the lunar surface. Neil Armstrong and Buzz Aldrin spent 22 hours exploring, while Mike Collins remained in orbit.

- During six manned missions, astronauts conducted experiments on the Moon's surface to learn about the regolith, rocks, meteoroids, solar wind, Moon vibrations (moonquakes), heat flow, and magnetic fields.

- Apollo 17 was the last manned spacecraft to land on the Moon. Astronauts on that December 1972 voyage spent 75 hours on the surface—the longest of all six missions.

- So far, twelve astronauts have explored the Moon's surface. Altogether, they have brought back 382 kilograms (842 pounds) of Moon rock and soil samples.

- Although both Soviet and U.S. lunar missions have provided great amounts of information, as well as rock samples, there is still much to learn.

- In 1994, the American spacecraft Clementine discovered evidence that ice may exist in a very deep, permanently shaded crater at the south pole.

Farside of the Moon

- The farside of the Moon is never visible from Earth. The first photographs of it were transmitted by the Russian probe, Luna 3, in 1959.

- The farside has more craters and only a few small maria. This is because the farside's crust is thicker, making it harder for lava to seep out.

- When the Moon's elliptical orbit brings it closer to Earth, it travels faster but continues to rotate at the same speed. This allows us to see a bit further east and west than we otherwise could. At other times we can see a bit more of the north and south areas of the Moon. These effects are called librations, and allow us to see 59 percent of the Moon's surface from Earth.

The Son of the Sun and the Daughter of the Moon

Russian Saami

Throughout the day, the Sun gives life to every living thing. The reindeer and the bear pull the mighty Sun across the sky as it throws sunbeams down to warm the Earth. By nightfall, the Sun is very tired and ready to sleep. One night the weary Sun got no rest at all, for his son Solvake complained nonstop that he could not find a woman to marry.

Tired of being alone, Solvake told his father, "I have traveled to Earth with a set of golden boots, seeking a maiden who can fly away with me, but I cannot find a girl light enough to rise into the sky."

The Sun was not surprised. He knew all of the maidens on Earth had feet that were too heavy. "You must have a mate from the sky," he told Solvake. "I have heard that the Moon has a new daughter. Although the Moon is not as rich as we are, at least moon folk can travel through the sky." The Sun promised to ask the Moon if Solvake could call on her daughter and Solvake shone brightly with anticipation.

The Sun and Moon do not always meet, but finally a morning came when the Moon did not rush off as quickly as usual. The Sun called out: "Hello, neighbor in the sky. I have heard you have a beautiful daughter. My son would like to be her suitor." The Moon was not fond of the Sun. She immediately hid her daughter with a cloud, replying, "My daughter is too young to have a suitor. She is not ready to be married and she will never be with your son. His heat is too intense and she would be scorched. Besides, she has been promised to Luminias, leader of the Northern Lights."

"Luminias!" shouted the Sun. "He is nothing but a wisp of light, while my power gives life to all things!"

"You are not as powerful as you think!" retorted the Moon. "At dusk you sink away into the sea. Throughout the night you are nowhere to be seen, and you only appear for the shortest time in the endless winter. The light of Luminias shines in the summer as well as the winter!"

Being compared to the Northern Lights enraged the Sun. He whirled and twirled until the sky became a savage storm of dark clouds, thunder, lightning, and terrible winds. "My son will marry your daughter!" he

shouted at the Moon, but she deliberately faded away.

The Moon knew that the Sun had great strength and she worried about her daughter's safety. As the storm raged, she looked for a place to hide her daughter. After some time, the Moon chose an old man and woman who lived in great privacy on an island in a lake. The Moon placed her daughter in a silver cradle and hung it in a tree branch, sure that the couple would find it and her daughter would soon be safe.

When the thunder, lightning, and wind finally stopped, the old couple went outside to look at the sky. They saw moonlight glowing in the woods and followed the light to the cradle. The man and the woman stood on their toes to peek inside, but the cradle seemed empty.

Suddenly they heard a child's voice, "I'm not here! Now, here I am!" They stretched up to look again and saw a young child glowing like a moonbeam. They named her Vanishia because she could vanish and reappear whenever she wanted.

The man and the woman treated Vanishia with great kindness. They thought of her as their own daughter, teaching her to sew reindeer hides and decorate with embroidery. Sometimes people from the other side of the lake would catch a glimpse of Vanishia. They began to talk about the mysterious beauty of the young maiden.

Eventually, the Sun heard about the grace and charm of the island girl. Even though it was doubtful any girl on Earth would ever fly, the Sun told Solvake to take his golden boots and seek her out.

Solvake flew over the island and spotted Vanishia on the shore of the lake. Wasting no time, he landed beside her on the sand. Gazing into the beautiful face of the startled maiden, Solvake fell in love. He boldly announced, "I am the son of the Sun!" and held out his golden boots. "Try these on!" he ordered.

Vanishia accepted the golden boots and pushed her feet inside, but they were so hot her skin began to burn. "They are too hot!" she cried out, but Solvake did not think that mattered, for his love was selfish.

"You will get used to the heat," he insisted. "You must come with me." He reached out to Vanishia, but not quickly enough. She had already said, "I am not here!" and disappeared.

Vanishia hid in the woods until her mother appeared at nightfall. The Moon slowly rose, lighting the way for her daughter to find her way away from the lake, over barren plains, to a little house by the ocean. The small house was not very clean, so Vanishia got a bucket of water and some rags, scrubbing until she became too tired to work any longer. Crawling inside a trunk, Vanishia pulled a blanket over her shoulders and fell into a deep sleep.

She awoke when the door of the house swung open and warriors glistening with silver clattered noisily into the room. They were the Northern Lights brothers, led by the oldest and most handsome brother, Luminias. As they ate their meal, Luminias noticed the changes in the room. "Someone has cleaned our home," he said to his brothers. "I feel we are being watched." They looked about the room but, seeing nothing, continued to eat.

When they were finished their meal, the warriors took up their sabers, swords, and shields, rose up into the sky, and played out a mock battle. Streaks of light and flashes of color glowed from their weapons, until finally they danced across the sky toward the sea. One warrior remained behind. It was Luminias. He went inside the house and called: "I know someone is here. Please show yourself to me."

Vanishia allowed herself to be visible and they fell deeply in love. Vanishia and Luminias were married in the moonlight that very night.

From that time on, Luminias spent his days with Vanishia, leaving at sunset with his brothers to travel to the ocean and raise his sword in the sky. Vanishia was happy but longed for more time with her husband. She asked him to spend a night with her, as well as the day, but he insisted he must return to the nightly battle in the sky.

Vanishia did not give up on her wish. She sewed a reindeer cloth into a curtain, embroidering it with a sun so bright it seemed to stream with light. One day, she waited until Luminias slept, then carefully hung the reindeer cloth over a window. Luminias woke up and looked at the window. He thought the Sun was still high in the sky and made no attempt to leave.

Almost the entire night passed before Luminias finally opened the door of the house. He was very surprised to see the Sun about to rise and ran into the yard to find his brothers. The rising Sun saw Luminias and vengefully shot a fiery arrow at his heart. The shaft found its mark. Vanishia ran to help her husband, but it was too late. His spirit rose into the sky above the ocean.

The Sun turned to Vanishia. "Now you will marry my son!" he roared, his fiery breath scorching the poor maiden. "Never," Vanishia cried. "I will not marry Solvake!" Enraged, the flaring Sun grabbed her by the hair and flung her high into the sky.

The Moon caught Vanishia and held her tight. The shadow of Vanishia's face can still be seen on the Moon to this day, as she watches the Northern Lights and dreams of Luminias.

HALOS AND MOONBOWS

A ring of light around the Moon is called a lunar halo, and is most likely to occur when the Moon is within a few days of the Full phase. Very high cirrus clouds containing the right-sized, six-sided ice crystals must be present in Earth's atmosphere. The halo is caused when moonlight is refracted (bent) through the ice crystals. You may only see part of a halo or you may see a short arc or pillar of light to the side of the Moon, called a moondog.

A moonbow is an arc of light, like a rainbow, but is perceived as white because of our eyes' poor ability to see colors in dim light. They rarely occur and can only be seen with your back facing the Moon, on bright moonlit nights. Moonbows are created when ice crystals refract moonlight.

NATIVE NORTH AMERICAN MOON NAMES

In ancient times, North American Native peoples learned how to keep track of time by paying attention to the phases of the Moon. They also noticed that there was one day every spring when sunlight and darkness were of equal length. This day occurs in March when the Sun crosses the plane of Earth's equator, while moving northward. Called the spring equinox, this became the beginning of the Native calendar.

Early North American Native peoples used the Moon to know when to plant, when to harvest, and when to hunt. They noticed they could see 12 or 13 full Moons in one year. Although various tribes had different names for each Full Moon, Algonquin Natives of eastern regions of North America generally recognized the following names, which were accepted and added to by European settlers:

January: Wolf Moon—wolf packs howl in the season of cold and deep snow

February: Hunger Moon—harsh weather makes it hard to hunt

March: Worm Moon—the ground begins to thaw and earthworm casts appear

April: Pink Moon—a pink flower called wild ground phlox is common

May: Flower Moon—many species of flowers are in bloom

June: Strawberry Moon—the month to pick strawberries

July: Thunder Moon—the month that most often has thunderstorms

August: Fruit Moon or Barley Moon—the names used for a late August or early September Moon, in the years that the Harvest Moon occurs in late September or early October

September or October: Harvest Moon—the Moon casts so much light, food can be gathered at night

October: Hunter's Moon—the leaves have fallen and it is time to hunt

November: Beaver Moon—the beavers are getting ready for winter

December: Cold Moon—the nights are long and dark

Anansi's Rescue from the River
West African

Once upon a time, a clever trickster known as Anansi lived with the Ashanti in the part of West Africa known as Ghana. Anansi had special powers because his father was Nyame, the sky god, and his mother was Asase Ya, the mother of the gods. She was also the Ashanti Earth and fertility goddess. Anansi is believed to have created the first man, who became alive when Nyame breathed him into life. Anansi has been called the creator of the Sun, Moon, and stars.

When times were good, Anansi lived as a man in a village. But when faced with danger or not enough food, Anansi used his powers to become a cunning spider with the ability to best all other creatures with his crafty ploys.

When Anansi's first son was born, he wished to give him a good name. Before he could state his choice, the infant spider spoke, saying, "I have a name. It is Akakai, which means See Trouble." It was a good name, for his eyes were so large they seemed to take over his entire face.

The second son also arrived with a name. He said, "I am called Twa Akwan, which means Road Builder."

The third son announced, "I am Hwe Nsuo—River Drinker." His mouth was so big that when he walked he looked like a mouth with eight legs.

The fourth called himself Adwafo— Game Skinner. The fifth was Toto Abuo—Stone Thrower. The last son was Da Yi Ya, which means Lie on the Ground Like a Cushion. He had been short and fat since birth.

One day, Anansi told his wife and sons that he must go on a long trip and be away for several weeks. His family did not know how he was until See Trouble announced, "Father is far away in the middle of the jungle! He has fallen into a river and needs our help!" Road Builder immediately began building a road that would lead them to Anansi. The other five sons followed the road through the jungle until at last they reached the river's edge.

River Drinker leaned down to the shoreline and opened his enormous mouth. Water rushed inside until he had swallowed the river dry. Still they did not see Anansi, but they did see a very large fish. They thought Anansi must be inside the fish, so Game Skinner cut him open. Sure enough, Anansi stepped out, but immediately faced more danger!

A falcon diving toward the spiders swooped down to Anansi and caught him in its beak. As the falcon soared up into the sky, Stone Thrower reached for a rock. He took careful aim and threw the rock at the falcon. It struck the bird and it dropped Anansi, but now the poor spider was falling toward the Earth at a frightening speed.

Just before Anansi hit the ground, Lie on the Ground Like a Cushion dove beneath his father and broke his fall with his soft body. Anansi was saved and the six sons returned to the village without anything else going wrong.

On Anansi's first night home, he looked out into the forest and noticed something shining. It was round and white and glowed with a silver light more glorious than anything he had ever seen. The treasure Anansi discovered was the Moon.

Anansi decided to give the Moon to the son who had done the most to rescue him during his dangerous journey. He called his children together and showed them the precious gift. Each son wanted it for himself and argued that he deserved it more than the others. See Trouble insisted that if it were not for him, his brothers would not have been able to help Anansi. Road Builder argued that without his help, they would not have reached the river. River Drinker pointed out that Anansi would still be lost if he had not

swallowed the entire river. Game Skinner argued that their father would have had to remain inside the fish if he had not been there to release him. Stone Thrower reminded them of the falcon that was carrying Anansi away, before he skillfully threw the rock. Lie on the Ground Like a Cushion insisted Anansi would not be alive if he had not broken his fall.

Each son was right and none agreed to give up his chance to own the Moon. They squabbled and argued and bickered. They called each other names and shoved each other back and forth, each son intent on convincing the others of his importance.

Anansi asked his father, Nyame, to help him choose one of his sons. The sky god watched the brothers feud. He listened to them long into the night, until he saw a tinge of light on the eastern horizon. Nyame felt impatient when he realized how much time had been wasted quarreling over the Moon. He decided none of the brothers should have it. Reaching down from the sky, Nyame heaved the Moon upward with all his might. It sailed up, over the trees of the forest, and beyond the clouds, until it was high above the horizon.

From that time, the Moon has circled the Earth for all to see and admire.

Observing the Moon

- No more than 50 percent of the Full Moon's surface can be seen at one time.

- The best place to look for detailed features of the Moon is the terminator—the line that separates the dark and bright portions of the Moon.

- Early astronomers thought the large lava-filled basins on the Moon were full of water and named them after the Latin word for seas, *maria*. Today we know that there are no seas on the Moon. Maria can be seen as dark, flat areas. The brighter areas on the Moon are called terrae or highlands and cover about 85 percent of the Moon's surface.

- Use binoculars to observe craters and mountain ranges when the Moon is near a Quarter phase and shadows are long.

- Bright rays like wheel spokes can be seen radiating from some of the Moon's youngest craters, and they usually contain small craters of their own. They have been examined by astronauts and are described as thin surface deposits associated with younger craters.

- The rays can be most clearly seen during a Full Moon when there are no shadows and the Moon looks "flat."

A long time ago, an old woman lived with her two children in the mountains. Because her husband had died, she worked for a wealthy nobleman in the nearest village. One day, when it was time to go home, the old woman was given a box of buckwheat puddings. She put the puddings in a basket, placed the basket on her head, and hurried out of the nobleman's house. The children would be hungry and she was anxious to go home and feed them.

Leaving the village behind, she followed the dirt path that rose up the steep hills to home. The woman chose her steps carefully, steadying the basket now and then to prevent the precious food from falling. She was imagining all the things she would do that evening, when an animal sprang onto the path and blocked her way. It was a tiger, with a big mouth, sharp teeth, and a very menacing growl.

"Old woman!" demanded the tiger, "What is in that basket?"

"It is full of buckwheat puddings for my children," she answered.

"Give me one or I will have you for supper!" growled the tiger.

The frightened woman handed him a pudding and rushed off as the tiger devoured the food. When she came to the next hill, the tiger once again blocked her path.

"Old woman, give me some more pudding!" he growled.

She took the basket off her head and handed him another pudding. As the tiger ate, she put the basket back on her head and hurried along the path to her house. She hoped she had seen the last of the thieving animal, but again and again the tiger ran ahead through the forest, only to reappear and block her way. Finally, all the puddings were gone and when he stopped her yet again, she shouted, "I have no more puddings to feed you. Go on your way, greedy tiger."

But the tiger would not leave her alone. "Give me your arms or I will eat every last bit of you!" he demanded. She let him have her arms and continued walking, but once again the tiger ran ahead and would not let her pass.

"Give me your legs or I will eat every last bit of you!" he roared.

"How will I get home?" cried the woman, but the tiger did not care. To save her life, the woman gave him her legs. As he ate, she tried to get away by rolling down the path. But still the tiger was not content! He soon caught up and landed next to her with a mighty leap. Without a word of warning, the tiger gobbled up the rest of the woman until there was nothing left but a pile of clothes.

All this time, the two children waited outside for their mother to come home. When the sky darkened, they went inside and locked the door. She had warned them many times to be careful of the tigers that roamed the mountains. The children were very hungry, but since there was nothing to eat, they lay down on the floor to rest.

Back in the forest, the tiger thought about his tasty supper and decided that the old woman's children would make a wonderful dessert. He put on her dress, tied a white handkerchief over his head, and walked on his hind legs to the house. Knocking on the door, the tiger called out in his best old lady voice, "Open the door, dear children. I have brought some wonderful buckwheat puddings for your supper."

The children were not sure whether or not they should open the door. Their mother had often reminded them to think for themselves. They called through the wooden door. "Mother, is that really you? Your voice sounds different."

"Yes, my voice is hoarse," the clever tiger replied. "I have been shouting at sparrows all day. They kept trying to steal the barley as it dried." Once again, the children did not know whether or not to believe the voice.

"Why don't you put your arm through the hole in the door so we can see that it is really you?" asked the children. The tiger put one of his paws through the door and the children reached out to touch it.

"Your arm is very rough!" exclaimed the children, but once again the clever tiger had an answer. "I did the laundry today and used rice paste to starch the clothes. That is why my arm is rough."

The children did not believe the voice and peered through the hole in the door. They saw a tiger dressed in clothes, and although they were very surprised, they did not say anything. Without a sound, the children dashed to the other side of the house and slipped out the back door into the darkness. They climbed a tall tree, perched on some branches, and hid among the leaves, hoping the tiger would give up and leave.

The tiger called out to the children again, but since they would not answer, he broke down the door and searched the house. Roaring angrily, the tiger circled outside, determined to scare the children from their hiding place. He searched all night, but the children were so quiet he could not find them. At last, toward dawn, the frustrated tiger flopped down beside the well and waited for morning. When light finally crept over the horizon, the tiger peered down the rough hole of the well. He saw the reflections of the children in the water and pretended once more to be their mother: "You poor children have fallen down the well. How can I help you out?"

The children laughed at the foolish tiger. Hearing their giggles, he looked up and realized they were in the tree. "Oh!" exclaimed the tiger. "You are stuck in the tree! What can I do to help you down?"

"Spread some sesame oil on the tree trunk," called the children, "to make it easy to climb." The tiger brought some sesame oil from the house and rubbed it on the trunk, but he could not climb up because it was so slippery.

The tiger was angry now, but kept his voice pleasant. "You are such clever children! Tell me how you managed to climb so high up the tree."

The children replied, "It's very easy. All you have to do is make notches in the trunk with an ax. That makes it easy to climb as high as you want." The tiger found an ax by the woodpile and began to make footholds in the trunk.

The terrified children realized they needed help to escape the tiger. They prayed to the God of Heaven: "If we are worthy, please save us by sending down the Heavenly Iron Chain, but if it is our time to die, please send down the Rotten Straw Rope." The Heavenly Iron Chain immediately came down from the sky. The children grabbed onto it and held tight as it raised them into the Heavenly Kingdom.

The hungry tiger was not ready to give up and decided to copy the children by praying, too. Worried the God of Heaven would not find him worthy because of his trickery, the tiger changed the words of the prayer.

"Dear God in Heaven," he said, "If I am worthy, please send down the Rotten Straw Rope. If I am not meant to live, please send me the Heavenly Iron Chain." He believed that by saying the words this way, he would get what he really wanted—the Heavenly Iron Chain.

The tiger did not know that praying was enough to make the gods consider him worthy. They lowered the Rotten Straw Rope and the anxious tiger grabbed it and climbed upward without looking at it very closely. Halfway up, the line broke. The tiger fell to Earth, crashing into a broom-corn field and breathing his last breath. The sharp corn stems pierced his skin and splattered the leaves with blood. Broom-corn leaves have had bright red spots since that day.

The children lived safe from harm in the Heavenly Kingdom until the King told them they could no longer be idle. "You shall be the Sun," he told the boy, "and light the Earth each day." He turned to the girl and said, "You shall be the Moon and light the world at night." The girl protested, "I do not like the night! Wouldn't my brother be a better Moon?" The King agreed and the girl became the Sun and the boy became the Moon. The girl was very shy and felt embarrassed when people stared at her in the sky. She solved this by shining so brightly, no one could look directly at her face.

The Closest Dot in the Sky

Since the first humans walked upon the Earth, people from all parts of the world gazed up at the Moon and created the stories we know. These tales allow us to go back in time, look into the minds of ancient people, and imagine what their world was like.

The myths were told orally long before they were written down and are much more than entertaining folklore. They connect the past, present, and future through stories that examine real feelings. Whether it is the virtues of bravery, loyalty, and honesty, or the curses of selfishness, jealousy, and cruelty, myths express the passions of our ancestors. The tales that portray these feelings reveal how ancient people viewed each other, their problems, and the world. The myths remain intriguing, for we experience the same emotions expressed in these tales.

The science of the Moon is just as compelling. People dreamed of exploring its surface long before the first Moon mission. Countries around the world continue to develop space programs that may involve more trips to the Moon and outer space.

Our closest celestial neighbor, the Moon is ever fascinating. Watch it change dramatically with different phases through the month. Look for it in the daytime and imagine the rocks, dust, extreme temperatures, and tremendous craters. Look for the shapes of the mythical characters on its surface and share the stories of the Moon from around the world. Have fun exploring the celestial night by Moon gazing...dot to dot in the sky!

Glossary

Apollo missions a series of American space flights dedicated to landing a man on the Moon and returning him safely to Earth.

asteroid a chunk of rock or metal in space, usually considered to be greater than a kilometre (0.6 mile) in diameter.

astronaut a person who is trained to travel in space.

astronomer a person who studies astronomy.

astronomy the science of studying celestial bodies, including distance, brightness, size, motion, position, and composition.

atmosphere the gases that surround a celestial body such as a planet.

axis an imaginary line through the center of a celestial object, around which the object turns. The ends of the axis are the north and south poles of the object.

bamboo a tall, woody, often hollow-stemmed plant that grows in tropical and subtropical regions.

begging bowl an object used by Buddhist monks and nuns for collecting food.

blue moon the second moon when there are two Full Moons in one month. When used as an expression, "once in a blue moon" refers to something that does not happen very often.

Buddha a person who has attained the state of perfect enlightenment sought in the Buddhist religion.

calendar month the months of the modern calendar, which describes each month as having 28 to 31 days. This method of tracking time fits the 12 months into the solar year—the time it takes the Earth to revolve once around the Sun.

celestial relating to the sky.

comet a celestial object of ice, rock, and dust that orbits the Sun. When comets pass near the Sun, they develop a tail of gas and dust that points away from the Sun.

cosmic ray a high-energy particle from space.

cowry shell the glossy, often brightly colored shell of a variety of shellfish found in warm seas.

crater a hollow formed by the impact of a meteorite or asteroid.

Crescent Moon the curved shape of the Moon when less than half of the illuminated hemisphere is visible.

Cyclops mythical giants with a single eye in the middle of their forehead.

diameter the length of a straight line passing through the center of an object, such as a sphere.

double-planet system a set of two planets of comparable mass that orbit each other.

eclipse the partial or total blocking from view of one celestial body by another. In a lunar eclipse, the Moon passes partly or entirely through the Earth's shadow.

equator an imaginary circle around a planet or moon that divides the north and south hemispheres, halfway between the north and south poles.

equinox the two times each year when the Sun crosses the equator, making day and night of nearly equal length everywhere on Earth.

erosion the process of wearing away by water, wind, or glacial ice action.

farside the side of the Moon that is always turned away from Earth, and therefore is not visible from Earth.

folklore traditional tales and unsupported stories and sayings that are preserved by a culture.

Full Moon the lunar phase when the sunlit side of the Moon is visible from Earth. The Sun and Moon are on opposite sides of Earth at this time.

gibbous the lunar phases between Quarter and Full phases, when more than half the visible hemi-sphere of the Moon is illuminated.

gravity the force that causes objects to fall or be pulled toward another object.

hemisphere any half of a celestial sphere.

highlands *see* **terrae**

kimono a long robe with wide sleeves, traditionally worn with a broad sash as an outer garment by the Japanese.

lava hot liquid rock from a volcano or deep surface crack. Molten lava turns to solid rock when it cools.

libration an effect that allows more than 50 percent of the Moon's surface to be observed from Earth.

lunar relating to the Moon.

lunar halo a circle of light appearing to surround the Moon, caused by the refraction (bending) or reflection of light by ice particles in the Earth's atmosphere.

lunar month the time between two Full Moons. This results in a lunar year of 354 days, which is 11 days shorter than a solar year.

lunar phase *see* **Moon phase**

magnetic field a physical occurrence that affects the direction of a compass needle. A magnetic field may extend from the interior of a planetary body and out into surrounding space.

maria (mare) the large, relatively flat, dark depressions on the surface of the Moon, which are flooded with lava.

meteorite a meteoroid that hits the surface of a planet or moon.

meteoroid a chunk of rock in space, considerably smaller than an asteroid.

Mi'k Maq Native American Algonquian people, mainly from Nova Scotia, New Brunswick, Prince Edward Island, and the Gaspé Peninsula of Quebec.

moon the natural satellite of a planet. Earth's satellite is called the Moon, while other planets' moons are given individual names.

moonbow a rarely occurring rainbow caused by moonlight refracted through water droplets in the Earth's atmosphere after a rainfall.

moondog a short arc or pillar of light to the side of the Moon that is often a component of a larger Moon halo.

Moon phase (lunar phase) the portion of the illuminated side of the Moon that is visible from Earth.

moonquake a vibration on the Moon that is similar to an earthquake, but usually not very intense. Some moonquakes may be caused by the impact of meteorites.

mortal unable to live forever.

myth a story used to explain an event, practice, belief, or natural occurrence.

naked eye eyesight that is not assisted by binoculars or a telescope.

NASA abbreviation for the National Aeronautics and Space Administration in the United States of America.

neap tide the lowest level of high tides, which occur twice each month, during the first and the third Quarter Moons.

nearside the side of the Moon visible from Earth.

New Moon one of the Moon's four principal phases. The New Moon is invisible because it is between the Earth and the Sun.

Northern Lights (aurora borealis) streamers or arches of light that occur in the upper atmosphere of the Earth's northern hemisphere due to energetic particles from the Sun.

nymph a beautiful semi-divine woman who lives in mountains, forests, trees, or water.

orbit the path of one celestial body around another.

penumbra a partial or imperfect lighter shadow found outside the darker inner shadow (umbra). It is the area between complete darkness and complete light in an eclipse.

phases the size of the luminous part of a planet or Moon, as seen from Earth.

planet a celestial object of rock or gas that orbits a star. Planets do not produce light, but shine by reflecting the light of a star.

plate tectonics a theory that describes the Earth's outer crust as made up of many plates floating on molten rock, resulting in earth-quakes, volcanic activity, and continental drift.

poi a Hawaiian food made of cooked, pounded, and kneaded taro root.

probe a satellite or other spacecraft used to explore outer space and transmit data back to Earth.

radiation energy from a heat or light source. Solar radiation is experienced as sunshine, a combination of heat and visible light.

rays straight lines extending from a common center.

refract to bend or change the direction of a wavelength.

regolith loose particles of rock that cover the surfaces of the Moon and other planetary bodies.

rotate to spin around an axis or center.

Saami the people of a borderless region called Lapland, the northernmost regions (above the Arctic Circle) of Norway, Sweden, Finland, and Russia.

samurai upper-class Japanese warriors who value honor over life.

satellite objects that orbit a planet or moon. The Moon is a satellite of the Earth.

solar system a star and the celestial bodies that orbit it. Our solar system includes the Sun, comets, millions of asteroids, at least 140 moons, and the 9 planets.

solar wind a stream of particles emitted from the Sun.

solar year a year based on one revolution of the Earth around the Sun, containing 365 days, 5 hours, 48 minutes, and 45.5 seconds.

spring tide the exceptionally high and low tides occurring around the New and Full Moon, when the Sun, Moon, and Earth are approximately aligned.

tapa a coarse cloth decorated with geometric patterns, made from pounded tree bark in the South Pacific islands.

terminator the boundary between the light and dark portion of the Moon or a planet's disk.

terrae the lighter-colored elevated areas on the surface of the Moon or a planet, also called highlands.

terrestrial planets the solid and relatively dense planets—Earth, Mercury, and Mars. The term is also applied to some of the largest and densest moons, including Earth's Moon.

tide the rising and falling of the ocean, caused by the gravitational attraction of the Sun and Moon.

trickster a mischievous character in folklore who enjoys fooling others and playing practical jokes.

umbra the darkest part of a celestial body's shadow.

underworld the place where souls went after death, also known as Hades.

waning when the Moon's lighted portion gradually decreases from the Full to the New phase.

waxing when the Moon's lighted portion is increasing to the Full phase.

will-o'-the-wisps lights that sometimes appear over marshy ground at night, often caused by gas from rotting organic matter.

Zeus king of the gods in Greek mythology.

Index

About the Author/Illustrator

Joan Marie Galat lives near Edmonton, Alberta, where she works as a writer on various websites. Her other books include *Dot to Dot in the Sky: Stories in the Stars* and *Dot to Dot in the Sky: Stories of the Planets*. Her next book in the series will be *Dot to Dot in the Sky: Stories of the Zodiac*. Joan has also contributed to a number of publications on a freelance basis, as well as writing for corporate clients. Her projects have encompassed speech writing, radio scripts, and exhibit text, as well as multimedia and animation projects. She was formerly published under the name Joan Hinz.

Besides writing and astronomy, Joan's favorite activities include spending time outdoors, picnicking, walking, cycling, swimming, rollerblading, and of course, reading! She has three children, as well as a budgie named Mango and a dog called Banjo.

Joan has been a frequent presenter at schools. She enjoys giving writing workshops, as well as sharing her knowledge of the night sky with students of all ages. Her website at www.joangalat.com contains additional author information, astronomy links, and fun for kids.

Lorna Bennett was born in Edmonton, Alberta. She studied Fine Arts in college and university, and has been working in design, illustration, and fine art ever since. She enjoys working in a variety of mediums, especially ink, watercolor, pastel, and oil paints. When Lorna is not busy working on children's picture books, novel covers, multimedia projects, and teaching drawing in elementary schools, she loves to mountain bike, read, cook, watch great movies, and plan where she would like to travel to next.